Steven Herrick was born in Brisbane, the youngest of seven children. At school his favourite subject was soccer, and he dreamed of football glory while he worked at various jobs. For the past thirty years he's been a full-time writer and regularly performs his work in schools throughout the world. Steven lives in the Blue Mountains with his partner Cathie, a belly dance teacher. They have two adult sons, Jack and Joe.

www.stevenherrick.com.au

Also by Steven Herrick

Young Adult

A place like this
Black painted fingernails
By the river
Cold skin
Lonesome howl
Love, ghosts and nose hair
Slice
The simple gift
Water bombs

Children

Bleakboy and Hunter stand out in the rain
Do-wrong Ron
Love poems and leg-spinners
My life, my love, my lasagne
Naked bunyip dancing
Poetry to the rescue
Pookie Aleera is not my boyfriend
Rhyming boy
The place where the planes take off
Tom Jones saves the world

untangling spaghetti

selected poems

Steven Herrick

First published 2009 by University of Queensland Press
PO Box 6042, St Lucia, Queensland 4067 Australia
Reprinted 2011, 2015, 2020, 2024

www.uqp.com.au

Typeset in 12/17.5pt Rotis Semi Sans by Post Pre-press Group, Brisbane
Printed in Australia by McPherson's Printing Group

Cataloguing-in-Publication Data
National Library of Australia

Herrick, Steven.

Untangling spaghetti: selected poems
Steven Herrick.

978 0 7022 3730 0 (pbk.)

For primary school age.

A821.3

Note: *toenails* from page 150
* The first four lines were written by a student in one of my school workshops many years ago. Unfortunately, I did not get his name. If he's out there - write me a letter okay!

To Jack and Joe,

With love, football and poetry . . .

contents

introduction

These poems are personal favourites from my three collections for children: *Poetry to the Rescue*; *My Life, my love, my lasagne*; and *Love poems and leg spinners*. Many of the poems in this selection were inspired by the childhoods of my two sons, Jack and Joe. As I write this, Jack is living in London and Joe is starting university. They are no longer boys, but young men.

Hairy young men!

When they were children, both boys would come home every afternoon from primary school and eagerly tell me about the events of their day. Because I was their dad, they also knew I'd turn their stories into poems.

Jack and Joe were so generous in allowing a house-bound poet to leave his desk and journey with them through the classroom and schoolyard.

We'd have afternoon tea of biscuits, cake and giggles before venturing into the backyard for the obligatory game of soccer. The boys would tell me about what happened at school. Joe in his quiet observant way. Jack would be much more animated, often adding theatrical flourishes of his own. From these stories, I'd create a poem the next day. When the boys arrived home from school that afternoon, I'd read the freshly-minted poem.

Their response?

Often giggles, but sometimes they'd frown and say, 'But Dad, that's not how it happened.'

Then we'd discuss the poem, or the incident that lead me to write about it and I'd try again the next day. Occasionally, I'd want to leave the poem as it was and I'd explain how it was saying something different from their reality. The boys would understand. However, I always felt that they were a little . . . disappointed. As if I hadn't kept my end of the bargain.

They tell me the truth. I write the truth. Poetry or journalism?

Of course, the best poems speak more than the truth. They take us into the emotion and joy and humour and the simple *thereness* of the moment. That's an awfully clumsy word for a poet to use. But it best describes what many of these poems are about – me trying to be with my two sons as they made their way through childhood.

It was the best journey of my life.

Steven Herrick
Katoomba, 2009

chapter one

house rules

digital clock

It's my first digital clock.
I'm learning to tell the time
(although I don't tell it anything).
At night I read in bed until
7:00
then I close my eyes
and think of the clock on my desk
I know it's slowly going
7:01
7:02
7:03
7:04
but I don't open my eyes to check
because I'm supposed to go to sleep at
7:00

In the morning I wake at *6:00*
although sometimes I wake at
5:52
then I quickly close my eyes
and pretend I'm asleep.
I don't want to upset the clock.
Sometimes I open one eye, just a little to check

5:56
No. Not time yet
until finally the clock turns
6:00.

I scramble out of bed
race upstairs to Mum and Dad
and jump on them as they sleep.
They wake, groaning.
Dad says, 'What's the time?'

I run back downstairs
look at my brand-new digital clock
and yell,
'6:02!!'

Mum and Dad don't need a clock.

They've got me!

coffee

Every morning
at breakfast
my dad drinks his coffee
leans back in his chair
smacks his lips
and says,
'aaahhh. I needed that to wake me up.'
And every morning Mum says
'why don't you use an alarm clock
like everybody else.'
And every morning Dad says
'because I can't drink an alarm clock!'

grandma

talks too loud
can't hear a thing
talks to the birds
each named after a grandchild
'that Simon's a worry, never eats a thing'
she says. not sure if she's talking about
a bird or a grandson.
buys pet plastic crocodiles
hundreds of them
sets them free all over the house
eats biscuits for dinner
banana on toast for breakfast
yells 'I'm 82. I'll eat what I want.'
the grandkids love her
write her letters she can't read
she writes back 'the birds are doing well'.
when they visit she tells them to
beware of the crocodiles
and to eat as many biscuits as they like
'that Simon's a worry' she says
as the birds eat, the crocodiles smile
and the children sing.

reasons we can't get a dog

We don't have a fence.
You wouldn't want him wandering off
    onto the road, would you?
We have nowhere for him to sleep.
No, he couldn't sleep on your brother's bed.
    All the snoring would keep him awake.
We have nothing to feed him.
Yes, you could give him your vegetables,
    but I don't think your mum would approve.
Besides, dogs scratch, bite, whimper,
    howl at the moon.
Yes, I know your brother does too,
    but we can't take him to the pound, can we?
And do you want the dog chasing poor Mrs Sims
    and her cat down the road.
Yes, it would be funny. But not for Mrs Sims.
And don't say you have no one to play with.
What about me?
No, I won't fetch your ball, roll over or play dead!
So, no. We can't get a dog.

house rules

When my dad heard my brother call me
'A dork!'
he said,
'Jack, we don't say that word in this house.'
So Jack walked quickly out the back door
stood in the yard
and yelled at me,
'You dork!'
in his best older brother voice!

the plants

the plants in our house have died.

not enough sun
not enough water
not enough fertiliser
not enough love and care.

too much thick gravy
too much cold coffee
too much stale beer
too many hanging toys.

the plants in our house have died
but what a life they had!

my three-year-old cousin visits the zoo

Look Mum a pekalin, a pekalin.
And 'dere 'dere
        a lion with a beard
        Simba Simba
        here Simba.
And 'dose pink birds
        big pink birds
        with one leg
        who stole other leg Mum?
And a big bear Dad
        he not Humfrey
        he not look happy like Humfrey.
And 'dose monkey
        scratchin' bottom
        funny Dad funny monkey
        scratch bottom all day.
I like Zoo Dad.
My favrite is horse
        with road crossing painted on them.

And my other favrite
is when elefant done toilet,
everyone laughed Dad.
I like Zoo Dad.
We come tomorra too?

smoke alarm

during the night
our smoke alarm went off
and off and off and off and off
and off and off and off and off
and off and off and off and off
and off and off and off and off
and off and off and off and off

until Dad hit it with his shoe

the ten commandments
[or ten things your parents will never say]

Let's forget dinner tonight, we'll eat ice-cream instead.

Goodnight children, I'm off to bed. Stay up as late as you want.

No homework tonight. I'm putting all homework in the fireplace immediately.

Children, don't be so quiet. Start yelling, turn the TV up, start arguing. NOW!

Yes, of course you can have 21 of your friends come over to stay on Saturday night. We've got heaps of room.

No, don't listen to the dentist. Lollies and biscuits are good for your teeth.

Yes, that SuperdoopaComputerGame is too expensive but let's buy it anyway and we'll put it in your room.

What's that? You broke the kitchen window? Good boy.

Can someone go to the shop for a paper? Here's $100, keep the change.

Yes, I know it's Monday, but why don't we stay home from school anyway?

names

I love my dad.
He says silly things
and does even sillier things
like . . .
he calls my brother and me
'Peter' and 'George'
when our names are Jack and Joe.
He says,
'Come on Peter and George, let's play cricket.'
We say,
'That's not our names!'
He looks confused for a bit, then says,
'Come on Alfred and William, let's play cricket.'
We say,
'Dad, that's not our names!'
'Oh . . .' he says,
'Come on Sarah and Emily, let's play cricket.'
We say,
'Dad, we're boys, not girls!'

'Of course you are,' he says,
'How silly of me. Come on Mark and Nathan,
let's play cricket.'

We go and play cricket.

names (again!)

My dad loves names.
He calls my brother Jack
'Jackie', 'Jacko', 'Jacket',
or 'Slack Jack'.
My name's Joe.
He calls me
'Slow Joe', 'Joe Blow', 'No Go Joe',
or 'Say it ain't so Joe'.
He calls Mum
'Darling', 'Sweetelbow', 'Pumpkin',
or 'My life, my love, my lasagne'.

I like his names.
So do Mum and Jack.
When we sit down to eat dinner
I call him 'Baldy two shoes'.
Jack calls him 'Big ears bullfrog'.
Mum calls him 'The man with two stomachs'.
Dad smiles and calls himself
'The wrinkled one in the corner'.

sarah's first words

Sarah's mum told her
the first words she ever spoke
were 'ball' and 'moon'.
She'd point to a ball
And say 'moon, moon'.
She'd point to
her brother's head
and say 'ball, ball'.

talk

Our dad never talks about his dad.

Grandpop died long ago.

We ask Dad about him
as we sit on a towel on the beach,
building sandcastles.
Dad shovels sand into huge castle walls
and fills the moat with sea water.
He carefully shapes each turret,
builds a bridge over the moat
as we talk about our work
and how Mum will be impressed.

My brother goes for a swim.
Dad goes with him.
I work on the sandcastle.
I know when I want to go for a swim
Dad will come with me,
in case the waves are too big,
or the undertow too strong.
I can see Dad and my brother out there now,
playing in the waves.

When they come back
I've finished the sandcastle.

'It's brilliant,' says Dad.

I go for a swim.
Dad comes with me.

Our dad never talks about his dad.
I think that's sad.

mum and dad are in love!

Our house is strange.
My brother and I have a bedroom
with four walls and a door
like any house
but
my mum and dad don't.
They climb a ladder to their loft
with only three walls
and a view over the lounge room
where the other wall should be!
In the morning when my brother and I play
in the lounge
we hear Mum and Dad in bed.
They start kissing
smooch smooch snuggle snuggle
they go on and on, it's disgusting!
Sometimes they whisper things,
soppy stuff like 'I love you'
then they start kissing again
smooch smooch snuggle snuggle.

It gets so bad
my brother and I start pretending we're them.

We don't really kiss though
we just make the sounds
smooch smooch snuggle snuggle smooch smooch,
My brother closes his eyes and kisses the air
whispering, 'I love you, I love you'
until I can't stand it any more and
I start giggling which gets my brother giggling
both of us rolling around laughing, smooching,
giggling, snuggling, smooching, giggling
until we look up
and see Mum and Dad
looking down at us from the loft
and Dad asks,
'What do you boys think you're doing?'

the snake

My dad says
to keep away from the woodpile
at the bottom of our garden.
Two years ago
my Aunt Pat saw a snake there
and every day since
my dad says
to keep away from the woodpile.
So why, every morning,
before he has breakfast
does he walk down to the woodpile
but
never bring back any wood?

my backwards dad

My dad
washes the car when it rains
mows the lawn when it snows
trims the hedge in a thunderstorm
sleeps during the day
goes to work on the weekends
stays inside when it's sunny
and eats dinner with his fingers.
My backwards dad
says hello when he drops me at school
and goodbye when he picks me up
calls me 'his favourite daughter'
when my name is Michael!
My backwards dad
feeds the dog cat food
and the cat birdseed
dresses as Santa at Easter
and says 'I love this song'
as he turns the radio off.
My backwards dad
is the best mother a boy could have!

after school

After school
my brother gets home
goes straight to the kitchen
and makes himself a
GIANT sandwich.

One piece of bread
two slices of salami
a few thick slices of cheese
Dad's home-grown ripe tomato
crunchy lettuce
thin slices of cucumber
some runny beetroot
grated carrot
raw onion (yuk!)
one more slice of cheese
some chopped olives
a thick smudge of butter across
the final piece of bread.

He places this monster
on a dinner plate,
pours a tall glass of milk

sprinkled with Milo,
sits on the veranda
and eats his GIANT sandwich
slowly
smacking his lips
and smiling.

Two hours later
when we start dinner
my brother says,
'I'm not hungry.'
Mum and Dad wonder why
but I know
it's because of the

GIANT

hiding in his stomach.
My brother, the giant killer!

my dad

My dad's a fireman!
So is mine!
My dad drives a sportscar.
So does mine!
My dad plays football for Australia.
Mine does too!
My dad has a beard down to his chest.
So does mine, and he has an earring too!
My dad has an earring and a nose-ring and a navel-ring!
So does mine. And my dad has a key-ring!
All dads have key-rings! My dad owns a Harley!
My dad owns two.
My dad fought in the war.
My dad won the war!
My dad has lots of medals.
So *does mine. And trophies!*
Yeah. My dad has medals, trophies, and he lost his leg, blown up by a bomb.
So *did mine. Now he has a wooden leg.*
Yeah, that's what I meant, only my dad has two wooden legs.
Well my dad has three!

Actually, my dad lives in another state, so I only see him at Christmas.

Mine lives away too. I never see him.

Hey, we should be friends. Let's forget about our stupid dads.

Great idea!

happy birthday 1

My dad loves me.
My dad loves me.
I know because
he rang me for my birthday
late last night
when I was in bed
and he told Mum
to tell me
that he loves me.

happy birthday 2

My mum loves me.
My mum loves me.
I know because
I wasn't asleep last night
and the phone didn't ring,
not once,
so Mum just said Dad rang me
to make me feel better
because
she loves me.

my grandma talks to birds

My grandma talks to birds.
She has a budgie
called Billy.
'Who's a pretty boy then, Billy?
Who's a pretty boy?'
When Grandma visits
she even talks to our budgie,
'Eat your seed, Sam.
Don't you look thin.
Eat your seed Sam.'
When we sit in the backyard
Grandma doesn't stop talking.
A pigeon lands on the clothes line.
'Hello pigeon, I'll get you some seed.'
A rosella perches on our wattle tree.
'What a beautiful girl you are, Rosie,
what lovely colours.'
A kookaburra sits on the power pole.
'Laugh, little fellow. Go on, laugh
your head off.'
Our grandma can't help herself.
Yesterday we went on a picnic
to the Botanic Gardens

where they have a big cage
full of galahs and cockatoos.
Grandma keeps talking:
'What a pretty boy.
What a pretty boy.
Polly want a cracker?
Polly want a cracker?'
Grandma stretches her hand,
holding a biscuit, into the cage,
and Polly
takes a big bite,
and bites Grandma's finger!
'X!#X+X!!! Polly.'
Grandma doesn't talk to birds.
Grandma swears!

the answer is no

My dad is always saying
'the answer is no'
before I can even ask the question.
Like last night
when Mum's homemade ice-cream beckoned
for a second helping.
I looked at Mum
and Dad said
'the answer is no'
before I said a word.
And later
when it was time for bed
and my favourite television show came on
I looked at Mum
and Dad said
'the answer is no.'
And this morning
when I tried to act sick
and miss school.
I groaned as Mum walked in
and Dad said
'the answer is no.'

It made me mad
so mad.
I put on my school clothes
without saying a word.
I packed my schoolbag
silently.
I kissed my mum
and reached to take my soccer ball to school
(which I'm never allowed to take)
and Dad looked up.
He was about to say the usual thing
but as I picked up the ball
I said, quick as a flash,
'do you love me, Dad?'

'the answer is . . . yes'
So me and the soccer ball
headed to school
with Dad at the breakfast table
still scratching his head.

wake up

I wake every morning at 6 o'clock,
my brother is still asleep.
I climb onto his bed,
I say in a soft voice,
'Jack, are you awake yet?'

He rolls over, still asleep.
I lean over him
and tickle behind his ear
tickle, ever so lightly.
He grunts
moves away
but stays asleep.
I tickle under his chin
ever so lightly
under his chin.
He scratches his chin
rolls on his back
and stays asleep.
Now I tickle on his nose
just lightly
on his nose
like a fly or a moth,

my brother hates flies and moths.
I tickle him again
on his nose
his ear
his chin.
Still asleep, he starts smacking his face
after the fly.
He smacks his ear, his nose, his chin
so hard
too hard
until he wakes and says,
'Did I kill it
did I kill it?'

What can I say but 'yes'.

One day I'll tell my brother
he should stop punching himself awake.

One day I will.
I promise.

chapter two

there once was a limerick called steven

advertisements for poetry

Buy Poetry,
New improved formula.
Chocolate-coated poetry.
A glass and a half of full-cream rhyme in every poem.
The taste that refreshes, drink poetry.
Poetry, don't leave home without it.
A poem a day helps you work rest and play.
Always poetry.
Ready for a change, try poetry.
Life would be pretty straight without poetry.
Take two poems and see your doctor if pain persists.
Start your day with a bowl of Special P
    (for poetry).
No added sugar, artificial flavours or colours poetry.
Everyone around the world keeps singing McPoetry.
It won't happen overnight but it will happen
    with poetry.
Lose 10 kilos in 5 weeks with low-fat poetry.
Poetry – it works for me, it could work for you too!
Try Poetry, today.

Note: Poetry should not be taken by people afraid to laugh, or those on a poetry-free diet. Nine out of ten doctors recommend poetry for a longer life.

a short poem on the weather

Thunder claps
lightning strikes

give me thunder anytime.

the poetry visitor

Yesterday
a poet came to our school
and read lots of his poems.
Some were funny,
some sad,
some even made Ms Stevrakis laugh,
        especially the one about kissing.
At the end, Ms Stevrakis suggested
we ask the poet questions about his poetry.
After a long silence,
Rachel asked, 'How much money do you make?'
Matthew asked, 'Where do you live?'
Sarah asked, 'How old are you?'
Tran asked, 'Can you speak Vietnamese?'
Sam asked, 'How come you've got a bald head?'
and Peter asked, 'Can I go to the toilet please?'

poetry

Ms Stevrakis says,
'Poetry doesn't have to rhyme
all of the time.'

She doesn't get it
when
everyone laughs.

She doesn't even get it
when
Sarah raises her hand and says,

'Miss, how much of the time
does poetry have to rhyme?'

But, ten minutes later,
during our quiet reading time
she starts laughing –
she laughs forever it seems

and so do we.

I didn't know poetry could be so much fun!

acrostic

A poem teachers make all the
Class write because
Rhyming poems are too hard
On our brains
So anybody, even a maths
teacher could write
In the
aCrostic style!

By Mr Sharp
(Year 5 Maths Teacher)

a limerick

there once was a limerick called Steven
whose rhyme scheme was very uneven
it didn't make sense
it wasn't funny
and who'd call a limerick Steven anyway?

another limerick

there once was a limerick about Mr Jones
but Mr Jones found it and

ripped

it

up.

a metaphor poem

Yesterday,
our teacher Ms Stevrakis
wanted us to write a metaphor poem.
Sam asked, 'What is a meta for?'
but Sarah saved the day
by raising her hand and
saying that a metaphor is when you say
        'Sam is a goat
        he is hairy and not very bright
        he's always chewing and making strange noises
        he lives on a farm
        and he eats anything!'
Tomorrow,
Ms Stevrakis is going to teach us onomatopoeia.
Sam said that if you put a mat on a pier
        it would get wet.
Sarah raised her hand again but
Ms Stevrakis said, in a loud voice,
        'Class dismissed!'
Sam said, 'What did the class just miss?'

love poem

Today Ms Stevrakis
read us a poem
on love

your lips are like cherries
ripe, sweet, and soft fruit
we kiss under a pale moon
we swoon
our hands clam tight
eyes bright
may this moment linger
I slip this ring upon
your finger
our lips, our hands
our hearts . . .

When she finishes
thirty-two students
who hate maths
put up their hands
and say,
'Please Ms
can we do maths now
please . . .'

spring

It's spring. It's spring.
the flowers are smiling
the trees are singing
the birds are
the birds are
the birds are birding!

but the grass is crying
        the grass is low.
for over in the corner is my dad,
he's about to mow!

in summer

In summer
when horses smile at the sun
and trees wave happily at everyone
when ducks waddle lovingly to the lake
and Mum on Sunday bakes a chocolate cake
when crickets chirp in the eaves
and raindrops glisten on the leaves.
In summer
when birds frolic and serenade the flowers
our dad, in his togs, is outside
    having backyard showers
the neighbour, Mrs Sims, calls the police
    to complain
about Dad, nearly naked, outside in the rain.

autumn

a tree without leaves
is like an old lady who grieves.

winter

yesterday
we built a big fat snowman
it was fun
but today
the snowman
ran
off
with
the
sun.

my dad is a poet

My dad is a poet.
He writes books,
and he visits schools
to read poems to the students.
This is what happens.

Front office.
Knock knock.
'Hello, I'm the poet,
here to read to your students.'

Oh the poet
and he doesn't know it?!

That's the lady at the front office,
she's making a joke.
Now she introduces Dad
to the Principal,
'Mr Watkins, here's our poet for today.'

Oh the poet
and he doesn't know it?!

That's the Principal,
he likes a joke too.

Now the Principal leads Dad
to the staff room
to meet the teachers.

Oh the poet
and he doesn't know it?!

Even the teachers
enjoy a joke it seems.
Now the Principal takes Dad
to the School Mall to meet
Ms Banbridge, the Drama Co-ordinator.

Oh the poet
and he doesn't know it?!

That Ms Banbridge is pretty funny.
And now the Principal stands
in front of all the students
and introduces Dad.

And the children all say
in their loudest, clearest voice . . .

'Hello, and welcome to our school.'

And that's why Dad loves children.
And hates rhyming poems!

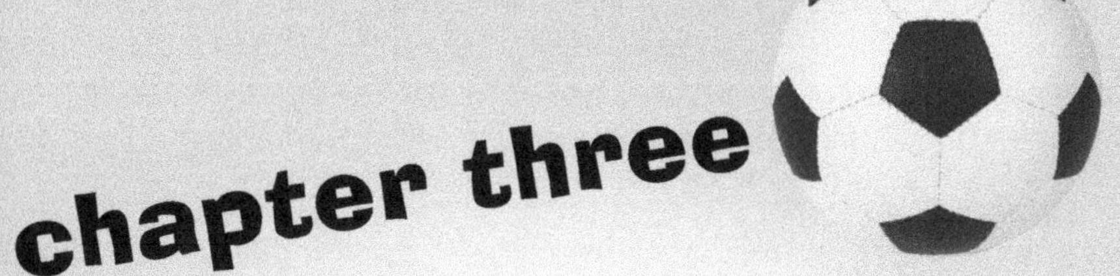

chapter three

the big Match

the big match

Dad and I won tickets
to the big football match
at Stadium Australia.
The Blues versus the Reds.
I was very excited.
I'd never been to a big game before.
We arrived early
and got a really good seat.
Dad bought me a hot dog,
a donut, and a drink.
He told me not to eat it all at once.
So I ate all the hot dog,
drank all the soft drink,
but left a little piece of donut, for later.
The Blue team ran out.
The crowd dressed in Blue cheered.
The Red team ran out.
The crowd dressed in Red cheered.
Then the referee ran out.
Everyone booed!
A man behind us said
something rude about the referee's mum.
When the game started

people jumped to their feet
and I had trouble seeing.
The referee blew his whistle
for a penalty to the Red team.
The man behind us said something
rude about the ref's mum again.
I hope the referee has earplugs.
When the Red team scored,
half the people in the stadium cheered,
the other half all moaned and groaned.
I told Dad it was like being at
a funeral and a wedding at the same time.
At half-time
I finished my donut
and Dad bought me another drink.
The Ground Announcer said that
anyone caught running naked across the field
would be arrested and fined by the police.
A minute later
a man ran naked across the field
chased by twelve policemen.
Everyone cheered the man,
and booed the police when they caught him.
Some people said rude things
    about the policeman's mum.
Maybe he and the referee are brothers?

In the second half
the Red team scored again
and some people dressed in Blue
started leaving the stadium,
even though the game wasn't over.
Near the end the referee sent a Blue player
off the field –
'for an early shower' said my dad.
I wondered what the player had done
that was so good
that he got all the hot water before anyone else?
The man behind us said more rude things
about the referee's mum,
then the game was over.
Dad and I walked slowly to the car park
and Dad asked me what I thought
of my first game of football.
I said it was fun,
but that the referee
spoiled it by always blowing the whistle
but what can you expect from somebody
who had such a terrible upbringing,
what with his awful mum.
I also said that the highlight was
the man who ran naked across the field.

Dad said he was a 'streaker'.
I asked Dad if we could go to a game of
streaking
next week.

i knew i loved her . . .

She wears baggy pants
and a white lace top to school.
She has ink-black hair,
tied in two pony tails.
She's the quickest in maths.
She can spell archa . . .
                    arhco . . .
                    acrho . . .
She can spell lots of big words.
She played the Queen in the school play.
I was her humble servant.
She was elected school captain.
I voted for her (twice!).
She knows the capital of Tanzania.
She knows who invented the telephone.
I ring her home – it's always engaged.
She knows the history of Ancient Egypt.
She knows how flowers grow.
I pick them for her – they die
      before I work up the courage.
But after all this
I only realised I loved her
when

during Friday's game
as the ball came across
she pivoted on one leg
and volleyed it into the net
and we won the Final
with that goal
and then
I was sure.
I knew that I loved her.

races

My brother and I play races in the backyard
We start with sprints
	from fence to fence
my brother wins, he's faster than me.
Then we place chairs and balls and boxes
	all around the yard
	for jumping over
we race, hurdling and weaving
my brother wins, he's taller than me.
Then we run from fence to tree
	climb up high
	swing down, land in the sandpit,
and run to the cubbyhouse, first one in wins
my brother wins, he's stronger than me.
Finally we race, crawling from fence to fence
	crawling under the tree
	through the boxes
	under the cubbyhouse, under the chair
and my brother loses, he's fatter than me!

I win. I win.
I'm going to represent Australia
in the 100 metre Obstacle Crawl Race
a gold medal for sure!

cup final

My team won!
My team lost.
My dad cheered and got drunk!
My dad cried and got drunk.
My mum baked our favourite dinner!
We had cold and boring take-away.
I went to bed in the happiest mood!
I went to bed [in my bedroom].
I dreamed of the winning goal!
I had a nightmare – the losing goal.
I can't wait for next year's final!
I'll wait for next year's final.
We'll win for sure!
We'll win. Maybe.

names

My brother and I play soccer
for the local club.
At the first training session
we all have to decide on a name
for the team.
Someone says *The Warriors.*
No, too violent, says the coach (our dad!)
The Devils.
No way, says Dad.
The Redbacks.
No, too dangerous, says Dad,
and our jersey is green.
The Greenbacks, says Sam.
Dad ignores that one.
How about *The Power Rangers*, says Peter.
Everyone looks at Peter as if he's mad.
What about *Manchester United*, says my brother.
I think that's already taken, says my dad.
The Killer Vipers, says Sarah.
Something less violent, says my dad, getting frustrated.
The Killer Bananas, suggests Sarah.
Everyone laughs, even Dad.
How about *The Bulls, The Chicago Bulls.*

No, this is Australia, and soccer, says Dad.
Everyone is silent, even Dad.

How about *The Marauding Marshmallows*,
says Sarah.
Marshmallows aren't violent, they're soft and sweet.

So that's our new name.
The Marauding Marshmallows.

What do you think?

backyard soccer

Me against Dad
Australia against Scotland
The Cup Final
I kick off
dribble past the tree
        past the house
        around the flower bed
and shoot . . .   GOAL!
1–0
Dad kicks off
dribbles past me
        trips over the ball
        gets up quick
        tackles me
I go down shouting 'foul!'
        I've done my knee in
        can't move can't run
Dad picks me up
        dusts me down
        gives me a big hug
        holds up three fingers
and says 'how many fingers am I holding up?'
I say 'three'

and Dad gives me the ball
I kick it between his legs
and run around him
and shoot . . .   GOAL!
2–0
Five minutes to go
I dribble past the tree
          but the cat runs out
          I trip over the cat
          do my knee in again
Dad picks me up
          holds up four fingers
and says 'how many fingers?'
I say 'four'
he gives me the ball
I kick it hard
bounces off the house
into the GOAL!
3–0
Last minute
          Dad dribbles past the shrubs
          around the fountain
I tackle him hard
Dad falls down, holding his knee
          I pick Dad up
          dust him down

give him a hug
hold up two fingers
and say 'how many fingers Dad?'
Dad says 'sixty-five'
I say 'close enough'
grab the ball, dribble past the fountain
score another GOAL!
4–0
full-time.
Me and Dad love backyard soccer.

when my dad was young

My dad said
when he was a child
they didn't have computers
and he never watched television
and only went to the movies once a year.
He said
he spent all his time
having fun in the backyard
playing cricket with his brothers and sisters.
I said
it didn't do him much good
because
despite all those years of practice
he'd never won
a game of cricket
against my brother and me!

fair play

Yesterday
Sam, Sarah, George and me
beat
Nick, Kate, David and Chris
85 to nil
in a lunchtime soccer match.
Today
Nick and Kate are playing handball,
David's in the library,
Chris is climbing the equipment
and we have
no-one
to play soccer against.
It just isn't fair.

the big win

All season
my team lost every match
5–0
8–0
4–0
6–0
we never even scored a goal
1–0
3–0
9–0
2–0
until the last game of the season
against the undefeated top team.
Everyone was saying you'll lose
10–0
12–0
15–0
20–0!
But we proved them all wrong
because WE WON!
Yes, we won!
An incredible victory.
A complete surprise.

We won!
Our coach was so proud,
our parents smiled.
We can't wait for next season.
We won. We won. We won.

Oh. Did we mention?
The other team's bus broke down,
and they couldn't make the game,
so we won.

Yes, we won.

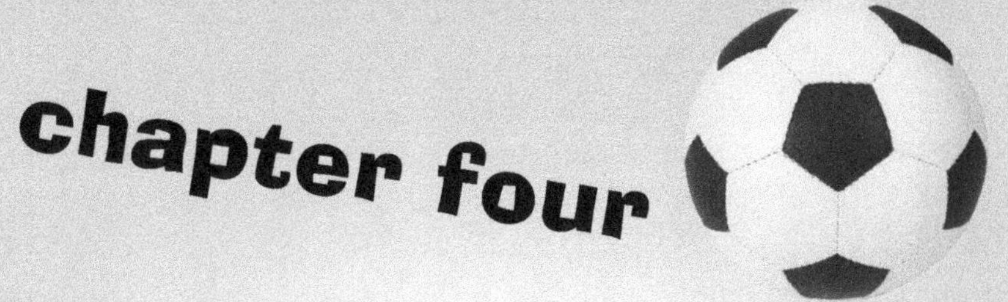

chapter four

Ms understanding

blush

At lunchtime on Monday
our class played *catch and kiss.*
All the girls
chased all the boys.
We ran faster than lightning
(to be caught would be frightening)
and luckily
no-one got nabbed!
The lunch-bell rang
and we all went back to class,
boys shaking hands and laughing,
girls saying, 'you wait until tomorrow.'
But at lunchtime on Tuesday
when our class played *catch and kiss,*
all the boys
chased all the girls,
and after a few minutes of running,
suddenly, as if by plan,
all the girls stopped
and we couldn't help but catch them
even though we tried not to.
The boys all panicked,
we'd won, and lost!

All the girls laughed
as we blushed
and vowed never
to play *catch and kiss*
again!

beetroot red

It's not that we wanted to kiss the boys,
we're not crazy!
But they acted so smart on Monday
laughing and boasting
about how fast they could run
that
Emily and I came up with the plan . . .
and it worked, like a treat!
And we didn't have to kiss them.
We just stood there
with our arms open
and our eyes closed
like we've seen on those dumb movies
my parents watch.
The big brave boys of Monday
screamed, turned, and ran
        red faces
        flashing feet
and when the lunch bell rang
we girls strolled back to class
laughing and poking fun

at the boys
walking far behind
blushing
beetroot red!

justice

He told a lie Miss
a whopping big lie Miss
he's in real trouble now
how could he say such a thing
he told a lie Miss
send him to the Principal
make him write 100 times
        'I must not tell a lie'
go on Miss
he can't say things like that
it's cruel, it's unfair
it's a lie Miss
a bald-faced lie Miss
a hairy-faced lie Miss
it's a lie
it can't be true
make him apologise Miss
lies hurt us all Miss
it's a l . . .

what's that?

Oh.

I knew he was telling the truth Miss
I just knew it.
He wouldn't lie, would he Miss!

the ten commandments (part two)
[or ten things your teacher will never say]

Children, pens down.
    Today I'm going to teach you how to swear.
OK, pick up your Textas.
    We're going to the Principal's office.
    We're going to graffiti on her walls.
Yes, good idea, let's stop doing maths.
    Let's have a sleep instead.
That's right, you heard me.
    I said no homework for the rest of the year.
I know you're all very hungry.
    Let's go get a pizza, I'll pay.
Children! If you keep making that awful noise,
    I'm going to let you all go home early.
This classroom is a pigsty, well done!
Today we have a special visitor to the school.
    I want you all to be as rude as possible.
Yes I know today was the science exam,
    but let's watch a video instead.
Don't forget, tomorrow is the last day of term,
    I'm taking everyone to the pub to celebrate.

how i broke my arm

I wanted to fly
or, at the very least,
stay in the air longer than five seconds.
So, it was either
        jump off the school roof
        which could be dangerous.
        I mean, I could land on someone
        or float away on a strong breeze!
Or
I could use a lever
to shoot me into the sky (but not too high!)
So Sarah and I got
        one long plank of wood
        two very solid house bricks
        and Peter Miski
        (the fattest boy in Year 5).
Sarah placed the house bricks on top of each other
and I laid the long plank evenly on the bricks
and stood on one end.
I told Peter Miski
to climb onto the fence and when I said 'GO'
to jump on the other end of the plank,
then I told Sarah and Peter to watch

as I soared into the sky.
(I assured them I'd wave,
and be back before lunchtime ended!)

I counted slowly to ten
and shouted 'GO'

and that's how I broke my arm.

childish

Ms Stevrakis was so angry with Sam today
she sent him back to Year 1 'for being childish'.
All afternoon
Sam sat with Year 1B.
The teacher read them stories about a steam train.
They sang songs about spiders
and they all counted to 60 aloud
(Sam gave up at 54!)
Then they had to do a drawing
of their favourite person.
Most of Class 1B drew their mum or dad.
Some drew Batman.
Sam did a very good full-colour drawing
of Ms Stevrakis, his favourite person
because she sent him to Year 1B
and made him miss a full afternoon of
maths!

the librarian

Our Librarian has long fingernails
and carries a brown leather bag
drives a bright green sports car
loves the wind in their hair.
Our Librarian wears smart clothes
        strong colours
        black patent leather shoes.
Our Librarian has perfect skin
and a long ponytail.
Our Librarian has sparkling diamond earrings
and a big opal ring that flashes
when they write on the board.
Our Librarian laughs a lot
calls us 'young lady' or 'young man'
never shouts
listens to everything we say.
We love our Librarian.
His name is Mr Johnson.

guess that word

Quiet, Class 5W
it's ten o'clock
which means time for
Guess that word.
Sitting up straight,
watching the board.
First one:
what word means 'old, infirm, or frail'?
No Mara, not 'Grandma'
no Phillip, not 'Teacher'
Yes, thank you Kate, 'decrepit'.
Let's try again.
What word means 'fat or overweight'
beginning with the letter O.
No Penny, 'orrible' is not a word.
No, good try William, but 'awful'
begins with an A.
Thank you Li, yes, 'Obese'.
Now finally,
what word means 'smart, bright, quick thinking',
a long word beginning with the letter I.
No Joshua, 'Idiot' is not quite right.
Yes Rebecca, 'Impulse' is a perfume

but it doesn't make you smart, bright, or quick thinking,
only smelly.
Yes Rebecca, I know your mother wears Impulse.
No Rebecca, I don't think your mother is smelly.
She may be bright, Rebecca.
Now, can we get back to the word
beginning with I . . .
No Matthew, 'Information Superhighway'
is not correct, and is two words,
but it was a good try.
Let me help. 'Intell . . .'
No Rebecca, not 'Intellaphone'.
No Sam, not 'Intellajokeatlunchtime'.
Please, Class 5W.
No Zwedil, not 'Intergalactic'.
Yes Yes Yes
thank you thank you, Tran
'Intelligent'
'Intelligent'.
Yes. Recess.
Go.
Now.

school rules

THERE WILL BE NO RUNNING IN THE HALLWAY.
    Or on the Principal's car.
NO BAD LANGUAGE ALLOWED.
    Unless spoken to a teacher.
YOU WILL RESPECT THE RIGHTS OF OTHERS.
    Inspect the tights of brothers???
SHOW GOOD MANNERS IN THE CLASSROOM.
    And bash each other in the playground.
RAISE YOUR HAND BEFORE SPEAKING.
    Raise your leg before farting!
THE TOILET IS NOT A PLAYGROUND.
    The playground is a great toilet!

lunchtime – an assortment of voices

Let's play cricket.
I'm batting.
I'm bowling.
I'm wicketkeeper.
I'm not playing.
I'll give you my chips if you give me your ice-cream.
I'll give you my ice-cream if you give me your
chips and a drink.
I'll punch you if you don't give me that bat.
I'll tell if you punch me.
Miss, who's your favourite Spice Girl?
I like Posh.
I like Spotty.
Very funny Miss, there is no Spice called Spotty!
I'll give you my drink if you let me bowl.
I'll let you bowl, but give me your drink first.
Jeremy says his sister likes you.
I hate Jeremy and his sister.
Well, Jeremy's sister's best friend Melissa hates you.
You go get the ball, you hit it over there.
I'm not getting it. I'm still running. I've scored 14
from that shot already!
Let's play football.

I'm striker.

I'm goalkeeper.

I'm still not playing.

I hate the Spice Girls.

My mum says Ms Dylan dyes her hair.

Let's go ask her.

You ask.

No, you.

Let's play cricket again.

I'm batting.

I'm bowling.

I'm wicketkeeper.

I'm not playing.

I'm still looking for the ball.

ms understanding

'Billy, your behaviour today
has been reprehensible,' said Ms Batlow.
'Thank you Ms,' said Billy.

'Billy, will you be so kind
as to lend the class your ear
for the rest of the morning,' said Ms Batlow.
'No Ms. Dad said I shouldn't lend
anybody anything
because they won't give it back,' answered Billy.

'Billy, is your brain
out to lunch today?' said Ms Batlow.
'No Ms, not for another five minutes,' replied Billy.

'Billy, put a sock in it will you!' said Ms Batlow.
'I can't Ms, I'm not wearing any,' said Billy.

'Billy, my patience
has run out!' shouted Ms Batlow.
'Would you like me to
go get it back Ms?' answered Billy.

cross-country race

Boys

Michael won by ten seconds
from Billy
who fell over in the mud twice
but kept going
because he wanted to beat Alex
who came third ahead
of Jason and Nathan and Paul
and particularly Sean
who took a wrong turn at the creek
and got lost in the bush.
That's why Peter who came seventh
got a special prize.
No, not for coming seventh
but for finding Sean
two hours after the race had finished!

Girls

Rachel won by two minutes.
Everyone else got in big trouble
because all fourteen other girls
dead-heated for second!
Anna told me why
but I can't tell anyone.
It's a secret,
but it might have
something to do
with the regional carnival
next Friday
where the first two placegetters
represent the school
and miss a whole day of classes!

marking the roll

Monday

'Good morning, Class 5B.
Time for marking the roll.
Anna?'

'Here Ms'

'Michael?'

'Here Ms Batlow'

'Peter?'

'Yes Ms'

'Alex?'

'Present'

'Sophie?'

'Here'

'Jason?'

'Here Ms'

'Sean?'

'Here'

'Billy?
BILLY!
Billy, why didn't you answer me?'

*'Sorry Ms Batlow.
I've changed my name.
Can you call me Horatio?'*

'Okay, Billy? I mean Horatio.'

'Here Ms!'

Tuesday

'Sophie?'

'Here'

'Jason?'

'Here Ms'

'Sean?'

'Here'

'Horatio?
Horatio?
HORATIO!'

*'Oh, sorry Ms.
My mum said Horatio
was a silly name.
So I've changed it again.'*

'Okay. Thank you.
Billy?
Billy?
BILLY?!'

*'Sorry Ms, didn't I say?
I've changed my name to Ulysees.'*

'Ulysees?'

'Here Ms'

Wednesday

'Jason?'

'Here Ms'

'Sean?'

'Here'

'Ulysees?
Ulysees?
ULYSEES!'

*'Oops, sorry Ms Batlow.
There's a boy in Class 2W
named Ulysees, so I've changed
my name to Wilberforce.'*

'Wilberforce?'

'Here today Ms'

Thursday

'Jason?'

'Here Ms'

'Sean?'

'Here'

'Wilberforce?
Wilberforce?
WILBERFORCE!'

'Oh, sorry again Ms.
My dad said Wilberforce is the
name of a town not a boy.
But I am here Ms.'

Friday

'Jason?'

'Here Ms'

'Sean?'

'Here'

'Billy
Horatio
Ulysees
Wilberforce
Adamson?'

'Here here here and here Ms!'

religion

Good morning, children,
I'm Mrs Bowen
your new Religious Education teacher.
Let's talk about God and Jesus.
Can anyone tell me
something good about God?
Anyone?
No Michael, God doesn't play
full-forward for the Sydney Swans.
Yes Michael, I'm sure he doesn't
even though your dad says he does.
God, children? Jesus, children?
Yes Jesus may have had a beard, Rachel,
and long hair and deep blue eyes.
Yes Rachel, just like a pop star.
No, I don't know if Jesus could sing, Rachel.
Yes, Matthew, God forgives us our sins.
What's that, Emily?
No Emily, now is not the time to talk about sin.
Yes Peter, God gave us his only son.
No Michael, God's son doesn't play football either.
Yes Michael, I'm sure your father says
'Jesus Christ' a lot at the football,

but that's not the name of a player.
Jesus is the son of God.
Well, yes, yes, Sarah,
Jesus did have a mother.
That was the Virgin Mary.

No, Michael, Mary and God
weren't married, not exactly.
Mary was married to Joseph,
but Jesus is the son of God.
No, it's not like *Home and Away*, Sarah,
where someone had someone else's baby!
This is religion!
God and Jesus and the Virgin Mary!
No Emily, we don't need to know
what a virgin is right now,
thank you very much!

Yes, that was lunch bell,
God help us.

braith the bully

Braith has no friends because
on Monday he pushed Sean over
and didn't say sorry,
on Tuesday he tripped Nathan
while playing soccer,
on Wednesday he threw a rotten apple
at Lucy,
on Thursday he spat a gobful of water
over everyone,
so on Friday we all kept
well away from him.

Braith had no-one to play with
so he played alone
until
he got into a fight with himself.

He lost.

braith (the bully?)

No-one will play with me
because they say
I pushed Sean over on Monday.
Well, it's true. I did.
But only because he walked past me
and didn't say hello,
not even when I said, 'Hi Sean.'
And they all blamed me
for tripping Nathan in soccer
when I only tried to kick the ball
but
I kicked him instead.
And no way did I throw
a rotten apple at Lucy.
I was aiming for the rubbish bin
and I'm a really bad shot.
And on Thursday I
wouldn't have spat water
over everyone if Alex
hadn't told a really funny joke
when I was drinking
and I couldn't help but laugh
and spit

at the same time.
And now
no-one will play with me
except this annoying fly
which keeps buzzing
and buzzing
and buzzing

OUCH!

I just hit myself in the ear
and missed the stupid fly!

I told you I'm a really bad shot.

the oval at lunchtime

At school today
Year 4 were playing soccer
on the oval, five-a-side.
It's tough playing
amongst all the kindergarten kids.
We keep getting in each other's way.
They're playing chase,
we're dribbling and passing,
and sure enough,
Peter Stuart, the biggest kid in Year 4,
runs right into a little kindy boy.
We all rush to help,
check he's OK,
and the little boy stands up,
rubs his eyes, over and over,
looks at big Peter,
looks at us all,
and says to Ms Ginola,
who's come to help,
'Teacher, arrest that boy.
Arrest that boy and
put him in jail!'

emily's love poem

Jason is so romantic.
Yesterday in class
he punched me on the arm.
He's so romantic
he punched me again at lunch.

I think he likes me.

jason's love poem

Emily kept looking at me in class
so I punched her,
not hard, on the arm.
She looked at me at lunch
so I punched her again.

I think she likes me.

science

Good morning Class 4W.
Today is Science Day.
Does anyone know any science experiments?
Anyone at all?
Sarah, any idea?

Yes Sarah,
    if we pushed Sam out the window
    he would fall straight down.
    I know it's called gravity,
    but it's not really something
    we can do today, is it?
No Sam, Sarah wouldn't fall faster
    because she's fatter,
    and we're getting off the subject, aren't we?

No Rebecca, we couldn't feed Peter twenty packets
    of crisps and see if he explodes.
Yes Peter, I know you'd like to try it
    but the answer is still no.
Come on, does anyone have any ideas?

No Matthew, we're not going to cut up live frogs.
And no Joshua,
    putting a whoopee cushion on the Principal's
    chair is not science
    it's Expulsion.
SCIENCE Class 4W SCIENCE
No Joshua, I said science, not silence
    speak if you have any ideas please!

Anyone?
No-one.

Well, I've got an idea Class 4W
Here's two glasses of lemonade.
No Peter, you can't drink one.
No Sarah, I don't know if it's
    Seven-Up or Schweppes lemonade.
    It doesn't matter, does it?
Yes, I know your mother buys Schweppes
    because it's Australian.
    So let's say this lemonade is Schweppes.
    Are you happy now Sarah?

OK.
Two glasses of lemonade, Schweppes lemonade
    and two cubes of sugar.

Now Class 4W,
what do you think will happen to the fizzy
        lemonade
if I drop a sugar cube into each glass?

No Peter, it won't blow up the entire school.
No Matthew, aliens won't jump through the window
        to drink the extra-sweet lemonade.
Sarah, I don't know what sort of aliens
        won't jump through the window
        and I don't care.
I care about science!
Yes Peter, if aliens did jump through the window
        they could teach us a lot about science.
No Joshua,
        I don't know if aliens drink lemonade.
Yes Sam,
        I'm sure they'd drink it if we asked them to,
        but I haven't seen any aliens today, have you?
Yes Sam,
        I know the Principal looks like an alien
        with his funny wig,
        but he's not from outer space,
        he's from Queensland.
Please Class 4W.

Science, lemonade, sugar cubes,
what happens?

Yes, that was the lunch bell.

Does anyone want a glass of lemonade?

After lunch we'll do maths.
That is, if the aliens haven't arrived yet.

ms stevrakis got married

Our teacher, Ms Stevrakis
got married to Mr Jones,
the Year 6 teacher.
Now, sometimes we call Ms Stevrakis
Mrs Jones,
sometimes, Ms Stevrakis,
sometimes, to make it easy, just 'Miss'.
Rachel calls her 'Mrs Stevrakis-Jones'.

Yesterday, at lunchtime,
when Mr Jones walked past our gang,
Sam said, 'Hello, Mr Stevrakis'
and everyone laughed
even Mr Jones.

chapter five

spaghetti jack

spaghetti jack

Jack loves his spaghetti.
He sits at his chair with a big bowl.
The first piece he hangs over his nose.
The second he drapes around his shoulders.
The third and fourth pieces of spaghetti
    he hangs over each ear –
    two dangling pasta earrings.
The fifth he throws at his brother.
The sixth he throws at me,
    I throw it back.
The seventh he gives to the cat.
The eighth he sticks to the wall:
    the sign of a good spaghetti.
The ninth he drops on the floor.
The final piece of spaghetti
    he holds up high
    smiles at Mum
    and eats it, very noisily,
    then he says,
'I'm finished! Can I have some more please?'

an american pie

Four score and seven years ago
our parents brought forth pies
(blueberry, raspberry, blackberry . . .)
and I was a thin man.
Now I'm dedicated to the belief
that all pies are created equal
before God and Man
and I eat them as fast as I can.

pancakes

Every Sunday morning
we go out for breakfast
to a cafe called Bon Ton
which Dad says is French for
'McDonald's only better'
but I don't believe him.
We always order the same meal
'Pancakes with real maple syrup
four servings please!'
While we're waiting Mum and Dad
drink coffee and talk about money
while my brother and I
chase each other
around the fountain in the courtyard
counting all the naked statues
three on the bar
one at the entrance
two in the tree
two in the fountain (one with spray coming out of his
you-know-what!)
and four on the walls
fat naked babies everywhere!

Dad calls us into the cafe
when our pancakes are ready.
Everyone goes quiet as Mum
pours the thick golden syrup
dribbling over the stack of pancakes,
then we all say
'we love you pancakes'
and eat them quickly
smacking our lips with the tingle of maple syrup,
    YUM!
We don't speak
we're too busy eating
our favourite food
as twelve naked statues watch us
and wish they were human
and could eat pancakes too!

'where's your homework sarah?'

It's my dad's fault Miss
and my mum's
that my homework's not done.
You see Miss,
Mum was working late
and Dad was fixing the car
and my brother and I were fighting,
    yes it was important Miss
    he said my hair looked like dead spaghetti!
So Dad came in to break up the fight,
and to make up
I offered to cook dinner,
fried banana and brussel sprout pie Miss
and my brother ate too much.
Dad said he wasn't hungry
and gave his pie to the dog
and before I could wash the dishes
and start my homework
my brother gets real sick-like
    and chucks up Miss
    sorry Miss
    I mean vomits Miss
    all over Dad's work clothes

and before we can get my brother to the doctor
the dog starts vomiting too
and howling real loud
like a ghost Miss
and he rolls over and plays dead
only this time it looks real Miss.
So Dad and I take
    my brother to the vet
    and the dog to the doctor
sorry Miss
    I mean my brother to the doctor
    and the dog to the vet
and we're there for hours Miss
and it looks like food poisoning.
Then we bring my brother and the dog home
only to find Mum's arrived
and started eating the pie Miss
and yes Miss that's right
she starts hurling I mean vomiting soon enough
so we all go back to the doctor
and by midnight
    everyone's home
    tired, sick, exhausted.

And that's why Miss
I'm sorry I didn't do my homework.
But Miss, Dad's cooking tonight
so I'll definitely do it for tomorrow
I promise.

the vegetarian

My sister is a vegetarian
and she doesn't let me eat in peace.
When I go to eat some chicken
she says,
'bye little chicken, bye Charlie chicken,
bye, bye.'
Then at breakfast
when I'm eating my bacon, she says,
'that's Babe's brother you're putting
in your mouth you know.'
And for my favourite, roast lamb,
she sings,
'bah bah black sheep
have you any meat
yes sir yes sir
it's in my brother's tummy.'
I'm getting so thin
because I just can't eat when she's around
especially when we have steak.
She says,
'the cow jumped over the moon
the cow jumped over the moon
and landed dead on your plate!'

We can't even have fish and chips
without her saying,
'the fish live in the sea
the fish swim in the sea
I don't eat the fish
And they don't eat me.'
My sister is a vegetarian
and the rest of us are on a diet!

my dad talks about cordial

When I was a kid
we weren't allowed
sweet things
like chocolate, and lollies.
We weren't even allowed cordial!
So, I'm ten years old
on our school break-up camp,
all of Year 5
and lots of parents helping out,
Wayne's dad at the BBQ,
some mothers making huge potato salads
and arranging all the cakes.
The whole class went for a swim
in the clear water of the creek,
played *Red Rover* for hours,
and ran around madly
like ten-year-old children should.
Then Penny's mum yelled
across the field,
'Come and get some cordial.'
I was very excited.
My first taste of cordial.
And being parents, they'd made lines,

one line for cups
one line for cordial
and one line for water.
Not knowing anything about cordial
this seemed very confusing.
Why did you need water
when there was cordial?
So I got my cup,
I stood in line waiting for cordial,
but when I got to Penny's mum
she put just a quarter of a cupful in.
I thought they must be running out,
or saving for seconds,
so I walked off looking
at my little cup of cordial
still excited about getting to taste it.
I sat down on a rock
looking at the thick orange liquid
and I took one big gulp

YUK!
It was disgusting.
Now I knew why there was a water line.
I quickly ran to the queue to
wash the awful taste from my mouth.
But when I got to the top of the line

Peter's mum looked at my empty cup
and said, 'Where's your cordial?'
I said I drank it and it tasted awful
and now I need some water, please.

Well, I never . . .
Peter's mum starts laughing,
laughing her head off,
and all I want is some water
because I can still taste the cordial,
thick, sweet, and gluggy in my mouth.
I'm about to help myself to the water
when she sees I'm upset
and she stops laughing
and whispers,
'You're supposed to mix the cordial
and the water before you drink it
you mad little boy.'

Now it all made sense.
So I went back to the cordial line
ready
for my first real taste
of cordial (and water!)

It tasted good too.
And I've never told anybody
about my cordial story,
until now.

especially the dog

We sit down to eat dinner.
Dad has steak and chips,
loads of chips.
So many they fall off his plate
on to the floor.
Our dog likes that.
Mum has salad,
no steak, no chips.
She crunches her carrot,
squirts her tomato
and chews her lettuce.
The dog keeps away from Mum.
My brother has mashed banana.
Some of it goes into his mouth,
some on the table, and
some on the dog's head.
My brother giggles.
I sit down to the largest plate of
mashed pumpkin and sausages Mum can make.
I dip the sausage into the pumpkin
and take big noisy bites.
Sometimes I tip tomato sauce
over everything,

even my fingers,
then I cry,
'Look, Dad, I'm bleeding, I'm bleeding.'
My brother giggles
and the dog barks.
Everyone loves dinner in our family,
especially the dog.

hunger

I'm looking at the clock
in class
while Ms Stevrakis is teaching geography
and I see
there's twenty-five minutes until lunch
and I'm watching Peter Miski
slip another Malteser into his mouth
and the sound that Ms Stevrakis hears
when she's writing the word 'Africa'
on the board is
                    my stomach rumbling
while the smell of cheese and vegemite sandwiches
comes from my lunchbox in the corner.
There's still twenty minutes until lunch
as I try and think of a country in Africa
but
all I can think of is
                    meat pies
                    sausage rolls
                    a juicy apple
and bashing Peter Miski
who's just eaten his fifth Malteser
                    right before my eyes

right before my stomach
and Ms Stevrakis is getting angry because
no one can tell her a country in Africa.
Then I hear Sarah whisper to Peter Miski
'can ya gimme a chocolate?'
and I raise my hand and say
'Kenya, Miss'
and then Sarah says to Peter Miski
'I'm gunna tell if ya don't gimme one'
and I raise my hand and say
'Ghana, Miss'
and everyone's looking at me, except Sarah
who's whispering to Peter Miski
'my brother Chad is gunna get you for this'
and I raise my hand and say
'Chad, Miss'
and all the class cheer
and I can tell Ms Stevrakis is impressed
because she lets us all out
five minutes early for lunch
and everyone races to their lunchbox
except Sarah
who races towards Peter Miski.

cooking

My sister said her favourite cooking was Mum's pies
My brother said his favourite was Mum's cakes
Dad said the best was Mum's spaghetti
I said the best was Mum's lasagne
Mum said her favourite was take-away.

the menu

I hate broccoli.
I hate potatoes, all mashed up and sticky.
I hate burnt sausages.
I hate those green bits in rice. Parsley, yeah,
    I hate it.
I hate cold peas, hundreds of them.
I hate stew with kidneys in it, YUK!
I hate beans and runny sauce.
I hate carrots and corn.
I hate cabbage.

What's for dessert?

I love ice-cream with chocolate sauce.
I love custard.
I love apple pie, steaming hot.
I love jelly, green and red.
I love pavlova and cream.

What's that Mum? Tomorrow you're cooking
Cabbage ice-cream with broccoli sauce.
Sausage custard.
Rice and bean pie, with parsley!

Carrot and corn jelly, orange and yellow.
And pea pavlova with kidney cream!

Please Mum, say it isn't true,
is that really tomorrow's menu?

chapter six

seeing the world

seeing the world

Every month or so,
when my brother and I
are bored with backyard games
and television, Dad says,
'It's time to see the world.'
So we climb the ladder to our attic,
push the window open,
and carefully, carefully,
scramble onto the roof.
We hang on tight as we scale the heights
to the very top.
We sit with our backs to the chimney
and see the world.
The birds flying
                    below us.
The trees swaying in the wind
                                        below us.
Our cubbyhouse, metres
                                below us.
The distant city
                    below us.
And then Dad, my brother and I lie back
look up and watch

the clouds and sky
and dream
we're flying
we're flying.
In summer
with the sun and a gentle breeze
and not a sound anywhere
I'm sure I never want to land.

marriage

I like our teacher
Ms Ginola.
She tells us about her husband Tony,
how he brings her breakfast in bed on Sunday
and flowers on Monday night
and on Tuesday they go to the movies
on Friday he cooks dinner
and every day he kisses her
when she goes off to school.
Over dinner, I tell Mum and Dad
all about Ms Ginola and Tony.
Mum doesn't say a word,
and Dad
offers to wash the dishes.
He's never done that before.

tantrum

yesterday
my sister threw a tantrum

(and it hit me on the head!)

patience

today
during maths
Ms Ginola lost her patience
but we were too scared
to help her find it.

the television news

On the television news
last night
we saw a man dying of hunger.
His eyes scared me
they were the same colour as mine
then he died, right there.
The reporter came on
standing in front of the crumpled man.

The reporter didn't look hungry at all.

wind

Wind tickles the leaves of tall trees
Wind groans and complains in winter
Wind is a flag's best friend
Wind takes paper, balloons and hats for a ride
Wind and walls have fights
Wind blows up girls' dresses [don't look!]
Wind sneaks under doors
Wind is summer's air-conditioner
Wind is a bully to little yellow flowers
Wind scares men with wigs
Wind howls at the moon
Wind and sail boats are in love
Wind cries, and cries, and cries
            then dies, until
Wind wakes, and whistles
            and shakes
            and shakes
Wind is a poem on a page
    that's here one minute

and

then

is

blown

away!

hugs and kisses

When I was five years old
my mum used to hug me
and she'd always say,
'You'll be popular with girls
when you grow up, my boy,
they'll all want to hug and kiss you.'

I'm eight years old now
and every time I see a girl

I run away as fast as I can!

the meaning of art

Sarah said to her teacher,
'I like green, it's my favourite colour.'
Ms Ginola replied,
'What shade of green?
The green of the trees?
The green of the grass?'
'No,' said the Sarah, 'just green.'
'You mean, the green of the leaves?'
    said Ms Ginola.
'The green of moss? Olive green perhaps?'
'No,' said Sarah. 'Just green. Green green.
That's what I like.'
'Green like your school uniform?'
    asked Ms Ginola.
'Green like the deep ocean?
Green like a lime, or a glossy green apple?'
'No,' said Sarah. 'Just green. My green!'
'Maybe green like your eyes.
Or green like a traffic light.
A bright smart green, is that it?'
    asked Ms Ginola.

'No,' said Sarah. 'I like blue.'

lost in the mist

I'm lost in the mist
I'm lost in the mist
I'm lost in the . . .
[Ouch!]   I just found a tree!

I'm lost in the mist
I'm lost in the mist
I'm lost in the . . .
[Splash!]   I think I found a lake.

I'm lost and wet in the mist
lost and wet in the mist
lost and wet in the . . .
[Yuk!]   What was that squishy thing
          I stepped in?

I'm lost in the smelly mist
I'm lost in the smelly mist
I'm lost in the . . .
[Help!]   I just heard a scream!

I'm running in the mist
I'm running in the mist
I'm running in the . . .
(Smack!]   I found the stupid tree again!

I'm knocked out in the mist
And it's worse than being kissed!

our principal

The Principal at our school is very old.
So old he taught my big sister.
So old he taught my mother.
So old he even taught my Auntie Pat.
When he sees me in the playground
he always says things like,
'You're not as big as your sister was.'
Or
'You're not as smart as your mother was.'
Or
'You're not as funny as your Auntie Pat was.'
But I don't mind
because yesterday when I saw him in the playground
I went up and said,
'You're not as young as their teacher was.'
I don't think our Principal
will bother me any more!

my teacher said . . .

My teacher said,
'If everyone's mum and dad
rode bicycles to work
instead of driving a car
the world wouldn't be so polluted.'
and Peter said,
'My mum and dad can't afford a car.'
Rachel said,
'My mum and dad can't afford a bicycle.'
Sam said,
'My mum and dad don't go to work.'
and Sarah said,
'Do you ride a bicycle to school, Miss?'

sarah's dad is famous

Sarah came to school today
and said,
'My dad is famous,
he was on television last night.'
We couldn't believe it.
Sarah's dad!
On television!
George asked, 'Was he on the news?'
Sam asked, 'Did he have his own talk show?'
Matthew said, 'No. I bet he won a million dollars
on a game show!'
Sarah kept shaking her head, smiling proudly.
Rebecca asked, 'Is he an actor in a movie?'
and Sarah said, 'Close, but not really.'
Chi-Soong said, 'He must be in a soap?'
Peter asked, 'Is he in a cartoon?'
We all looked at Peter.
'A cartoon isn't real,' said Chi-Soong.
'I know, he's in a football team on TV,' said Emma,
but Sarah kept shaking her head.
Then she told us to watch Channel 7
at 6:45 tonight and we'd all see her dad.
I went home and switched the television on.

I could hardly wait.
At 6:30 I started watching real close
so I wouldn't miss it.
The show looked very boring,
just people talking to each other about money.
But at 6:45
there was a commercial
with four men dressed in strange white outfits
so they looked like giant Rice Bubbles
and they danced around a huge bowl
singing,
'Snap Crackle Pop
I'm a happy Rice Bubble
Snap Crackle Pop
I'm never in trouble cause
I'm a happy Rice Bubble'

Wow! Sarah was right!
Her dad is famous.
He's a Happy Rice Bubble!
Sarah must be very proud.

toenails

Toenails are my favourite colour, green
Toenails are a very good source of Vitamin C
Toenails are what I throw at my sister
        when she takes too long in the bathroom
Toenails are what I eat
        when Mum forgets to give me lunch money
Toenails have fights with walls, and lose
Toenails make lovely sounds
        when scratched down a chalkboard
Toenails get painted on by my sister
Toenails kiss the dirt
        and sometimes take the dirt home for a bath
Toenails are the knife of a foot
Toenails get caught in the carpet
        and trip you over
Toenails hate shoes, socks,

and

falling

rocks!

anzac day

A day named after biscuits.
A day we don't go to school.
Mum and Dad take us to town,
          not to see the movies
          or play video games
but
to watch long lines of marchers
wearing uniforms.
Lots of soldiers,
even more than in the movies.
Old ladies crying,
little kids waving Australian flags.
Big brass bands,
drummers in funny hats.
Hundreds of grandfathers and grandmas
wearing their best clothes,
marching
straighter than I've ever seen old people walk.
Little kids no bigger than me
walking with lots of medals pinned to their shirt,
they must be very brave.
And these really old men
too old to walk, I guess,

riding in cars with no roofs,
waving, like the Queen.
Everyone's cheering and waving back
and one of these old men
        looks straight at me
        and I wave really hard
        and he winks!
When they've passed
and Dad picks me up
I notice he's been crying
but he's not sad.
I think, maybe
he's just sorry
the old man didn't wave at him!

flag

Grandpa says he fought for it
Dad says that some of it's not ours
My sister likes the blue colour
My brother says he wants to play cricket for it
My mum is sick of all the talk about it
Sam got in trouble
        for putting it upside down on the flagpole.
We sing songs at school to it
Rebecca thinks it would look better red not blue.
Me, I like the stars best.
What about you?

the drive

Today my dad and I drove into town.
We saw one fire-engine,
four semitrailers,
two ambulances,
and we drove faster than 158 cars
but got overtaken by
16 cars
and 2 motorbikes.
Dad swore at two old ladies
driving a Volvo
and an 'old codger in a bowling hat'
who wouldn't drive faster.
Dad wound his window down
to get some fresh air
and got hit on the head by a bee
who bounced off Dad's head
into the back seat next to me
and died.
Dad said he was very sorry
for the bee
and for the red mark on his head.
In town, we stopped at
6 red traffic lights

and drove through
4 green lights
and 2 yellow lights.
Dad turned the radio up loud
for his favourite song
which we both sang along with.
Dad swore some more when we
couldn't find a parking space.
I emptied a matchbox on the back seat
and carefully picked up the bee
and placed him inside.
At the Botanic Gardens
Dad and I gave the bee
a nice funeral.
We buried him near a gum tree.
I said a prayer
and Dad rubbed the mark on his head.
We both thought of
the
long
drive
home.

all the people in china

My teacher said
'If all the people in China
stood shoulder to shoulder
they'd reach all the way to Australia.'
And Sam said
'Miss, how do you
    stand on your shoulder?'

treats

Ms Ginola asked the class
to tell her all about their special treats.
Sam said, 'Pizza on Friday night.'
Rachel said, 'Horse-riding on Saturday morning.'
Peter, 'Potato crisps every day!'
Sarah, 'An ice-cream at the beach on Sunday.'
Nathan, 'A swim in the neighbour's pool.'
Tran, 'My own bottle of soft drink.'
Marilyn said, 'A toy. Any toy I want.'
Matthew said, 'McDonald's on Saturday night.'
And Penny said, 'A visit to the zoo.'
And Daniel thought long and hard
then said,
'I get to see my dad every second Sunday.'

the day the princess died

The day the Princess died
my family was driving
across the country on holiday.
The man on the radio
said
Princess Di was hurt in a car crash,
but her friend Dodi, and the driver,
had died.
I felt sorry for
the two people who'd died
but still glad that
the Princess hadn't.
We kept driving
and listening to the radio,
and the man kept saying
the Princess was hurt
but all right.
But then he said that
the Princess had died.
She wasn't hurt anymore.
She was dead.
Now I was sorry for
the three people who had died

as well as the man on the radio
who'd been telling everyone
she was hurt when she wasn't.

And all that week on holidays
everyone we met said
how sorry they were the Princess had died.
Some said how sorry it was that Dodi died.
No one mentioned being sorry the driver died.
We didn't know him,
but we didn't really know Dodi
or the Princess either.
And I began thinking
that if everyone, all over the world,
talked this much
about every person who died
anywhere in the world
in an accident
or of some bad disease
or in a war,
if we all talked so much
about each person who died
and felt so sorry for this person
and their grieving relatives
and we all felt so bad about it,
we'd get scientists and doctors

and politicians and journalists
and everyone to work even harder
to stop people from dying
and we wouldn't be happy
until we'd stopped all
unnecessary deaths.
That's what I thought of
after the day the Princess died.

a story of love (by uncle barry)

when I was young and treehung
shortpants and hairsung
I Maryhand got lovesick
we starrygazed and heartsquick
and giggleburst but lonelymissed
her fatheranger and mumcried
when loveincaught we could'vedied
but happychurch and marriedsoon
now playkids and smileymoon
we eveningtide and handshold
foreverlove we are heartsfold.

my son climbs trees

My son climbs trees.
He's like a monkey,
arms and legs stretching,
swinging,
grabbing the branches
as he climbs higher
until he reaches the top
where he sits
and yells,
'Hey Dad
I can see everything
from up here.
I can see the neighbour's roof.
I can see the end of the street.
I can see the creek in the gully.
I can see the schoolyard
and I can see the shopping centre, kilometres away.
I can see the highway
and all the trucks passing by.
I can see everything, Dad.
It's true.
I can see the forests
and I'm sure I can see the ocean.

I can see the outback
and the deserts
and I can see the Great Wall of China.
Yes, I'm sure that's the Great Wall of China.
And if I climb a bit higher
I'm sure I'll see the Statue of Liberty.
Yes, there it is.
I can see the world, Dad.
Come on Dad.
Come up and see the world.'

So I climb the tree
slowly,
scared to look down,
and I sit on the branch below
and my son says,
'Can you see it all, Dad,
can you?'
And sure enough
I can see the neighbour's roof,
the creek, the shopping centre,
the trucks on the highway,
and that haze in the distance
may be the ocean
or the desert,
and my son says,

'Can you see the Great Wall
and the Statue of Liberty, Dad?'
And I squint really hard
and I can see something
so I say,
'Yes, yes I can,'
although I can't really.
My eyes are too old,
my eyes can only see
what's in front of them
whereas
my son
his eyes are perfect,
his eyes can see the world.

retiring

Our teacher, Ms Batlow,
is leaving this week
after 40 years of teaching.
So on Friday all of Class 5B
give her a present.
Most of us give her a card
with 'best wishes' but
Sarah presents her with a painting
of Ms Batlow standing in front of the school.
Emily gives her some flowers.
Nathan gives her a box of chocolates.
Lorenzo gives her a framed photo of Class 5B.
Penny gives her a box of apples!
(Penny's dad owns a fruit shop.)
Simon gives her a pen in a special case.
Ms Batlow smiles at each present
and thanks every child
but when Billy gives her
his homework
all finished, neat and tidy,
for the first time this year
we all notice that
Ms Batlow is crying.

We're not sure if she's happy
or
if she's crying because
she has to mark Billy's homework.